JAPAN

A detailed beginner's guide to learn Japanese woodworking techniques, create amazing joints and carpentry projects

Joe Gibbs

Table of contents

CHAPTER ONE 4

    Introduction to Japanese Joinery................................4

    A brief history of Japanese woodworking traditions ..7

    Importance of joinery in Japanese culture and architecture 10

CHAPTER TWO 13

    Fundamental Principles of Japanese Joinery 13

    Overview of key principles...13

    Traditional tools and materials needed 15

CHAPTER THREE 19

    Types of Japanese Joints 19

    Mortise and Tenon Joints 19

    Dovetail joints 21

    Half-Lap Joints...24

    Through-tenon joints 25

    Other Joints...27

CHAPTER FOUR 29

    Step-by-Step Techniques for Japanese Joinery..........29

    Tips for Selecting the Appropriate Joint for Different Woodworking Projects 33

    Demonstrations of Assembly Methods and Securing Joints 36

CHAPTER FIVE 39
   Traditional Japanese woodworking projects 39
   Tansu Chest 40
   Chabudai (Low Dining Table) 45
   Magewappa Bentwood Boxes 50
   Sawhorses (Kigoroshi) 55
CHAPTER SIX 60
   Getabako (shoe cabinet) 60
   Irori (Traditional Japanese Hearth) 65
   Suggestions for incorporating Japanese joinery into woodworks 70

CHAPTER ONE

Introduction to Japanese Joinery

Introduction to Japanese Joinery is a starting point for learning about the rich legacy of woodworking that is firmly embedded in Japanese society. From ancient temples to modern furniture, the painstaking workmanship and structural integrity of Japanese joinery have fascinated artists and fans throughout the globe. Japanese joinery, which is rooted in centuries of history, stresses utility while also elevating woodworking to an art form.

Japanese joinery dates back to ancient Japan and developed with the country's architectural and cultural growth. The lack of materials and the necessity to build strong buildings that could resist earthquakes and other natural calamities impacted the art of joinery. As a consequence, Japanese artisans developed methods that emphasize accuracy, robustness, and durability.

Wabi-sabi, a Japanese concept that emphasizes imperfection and impermanence, is central to joinery. This mindset is represented in the workmanship of joints, where little differences and flaws are accepted as part of the completed piece's inherent beauty.

Traditional Japanese woodworking tools, such as the chisel (nomi) and the Japanese hand plane (kanna), are precisely constructed and built for unrivaled accuracy. These tools, together with a thorough grasp of wood grain and structure, allow craftspeople to produce seamless seams that are both practical and visually appealing.

Aside from its practical uses, Japanese joinery represents cultural virtues such as patience, discipline, and respect for materials. Apprenticeship under master artisans, known as sensei, is a time-honored custom that transfers knowledge and abilities from one generation to the next.

Today, Japanese joinery continues to influence woodworkers and designers all over the globe. Its enduring appeal stems not just from its technical proficiency, but also from its potential to establish a stronger connection between craftsmanship, nature, and the human experience.

An investigation of Japanese joinery provides insight into a centuries-old practice that goes beyond simple carpentry. It is a monument to the human spirit's brilliance and skill, reminding us of the tremendous beauty found in even the most basic joints.

A brief history of Japanese woodworking traditions

Japanese woodworking traditions have a long and rich history, dating back thousands of years. Japanese woodworking dates back to the Jomon era (14,000-300 BCE), when basic tools made of stone and wood were used to create everyday goods like cooking utensils and shelters.

During the ensuing Yayoi era (300 BCE-300 CE), advances in metallurgy brought metallurgical methods to

Japan, resulting in the creation of more advanced woodworking tools. This time also witnessed the birth of early architectural styles, such as raised-floor structures and thatched roofs.

Buddhism was introduced to Japan in the sixth century CE, bringing a wealth of architectural and carpentry expertise from China and Korea. Temples and shrines were built using sophisticated joinery methods, demonstrating the workmanship and expertise of Japanese craftsmen.

The Heian era (794-1185 CE) was a golden age for Japanese culture, with woodworking playing an important part in the building of palaces, temples, and gardens. Many of the fundamental concepts of Japanese woodworking were formed during this period, including attention to detail and harmony with nature.

During the Kamakura era (1185-1333 CE), samurai culture flourished, as did the building of walled castles and dwellings. Woodworking methods evolved, with a focus on practicality, durability, and protective architecture.

The Edo era (1603-1868 CE) was a time of peace and stability, allowing for remarkable advances in art, culture, and craftsmanship. During this period, woodworking thrived as new tools, joinery techniques, and architectural styles emerged. Kumi, or traditional Japanese woodworking guilds, played an important role in maintaining and disseminating expertise from generation to generation.

Importance of joinery in Japanese culture and architecture

Joinery is an important part of Japanese culture and architecture, acting as the foundation for traditional wooden buildings. Japanese joinery is distinguished by its accuracy, robustness, and flexibility, enabling the fabrication of complicated and long-lasting connections without the use of nails or screws.

Joinery is a form of creative expression in Japanese architecture, as well as a structural requirement. The complex joinery patterns seen in temples, shrines, and tea houses demonstrate a strong respect for workmanship and a healthy connection with nature. Each joint is meticulously designed to improve the overall appearance and integrity of the structure, resulting in a feeling of oneness and balance.

Aside from its architectural importance, joinery is profoundly embedded in Japanese cultural practices and rituals. Woodworking has traditionally been connected with spirituality and craftsmanship, and artists often take inspiration from natural materials and their surroundings. Woodworking is seen as a sort of meditation that requires patience, concentration, and attention to detail.

Furthermore, joinery exemplifies wider cultural ideals like simplicity, humility, and sustainability. Traditional Japanese woodworking methods emphasize the use of natural materials and little waste, reflecting a concept of living in harmony with the environment.

Joinery remains popular in contemporary Japan, despite fast technical breakthroughs and shifting cultural ideals. While modern building may use new materials and construction techniques, the timeless principles of Japanese joinery continue to inspire architects, designers, and artisans all around the globe.

CHAPTER TWO

Fundamental Principles of Japanese Joinery

Overview of key principles

1. Precision: Japanese woodwork is known for its exquisite perfection, resulting in flawless connections between wooden components. Precision is obtained by meticulously measuring, cutting, and fitting joints, generally without the use of adhesives or fasteners. Each joint is meticulously designed to fit together with minimum gaps, yielding a structurally solid and artistically appealing finished product.

2. Japanese joinery prioritizes strength, especially in traditional wooden constructions subject to natural pressures such as earthquakes.

Japanese artisans use interlocking joints and strategic reinforcements to make joints that are very robust and enduring. The strength of Japanese joinery is not just its structural soundness, but also its ability to uniformly distribute loads and minimize stress accumulation spots.

3. Aesthetics: Japanese joinery prioritizes aesthetics with practicality and robustness. Traditional Japanese architecture emphasizes beauty and harmony, and joinery is used to represent these values. From beautifully basic connections to intricate interlocking patterns, Japanese joinery methods are intended to improve the visual attractiveness of timber constructions while also complimenting their natural

environment. Japanese carpentry is frequently distinguished by clean lines, subtle embellishments, and an air of understated beauty.

Traditional tools and materials needed

1. Japanese joinery uses specialized tools designed for precise and efficient work completion. Some of the most

often used tools in Japanese joinery are:

• Chisels (nomi) are used for carving and shaping wood. They come in various sizes and forms to meet different joint types and woodworking jobs.

• Japanese hand planes (kanna) are crucial for smoothing surfaces and refining joints, resulting in a faultless finish.

• Japanese saws, known as nokogiri, have thin, flexible blades with a pull-stroke cutting motion that allows for smooth, precise cuts with minimum effort.

• Traditional marking instruments, such as scribes (kensui) and marking gauges (sumitsubo), are used to create exact measurements and guides on wood surfaces.

- Mallets (uchi) drive chisels and cutting tools with regulated force, resulting in clean and precise cuts.

2. Traditional Materials: Japanese joinery relies on locally obtained materials known for their strength, durability, and aesthetic appeal. Some of the most regularly used materials in Japanese joinery are:

- Japanese cypress, known for its straight grain, low weight, and inherent resistance to decay, is a popular material for structural components and finish carpentry.

- Sugi (Japanese cedar) is a common softwood in Japanese joinery, known for its strength, stability, and inherent insect repellant characteristics.

• Japanese zelkova (Keyaki) is a thick and robust hardwood used for structural components like beams and columns.

• Kiso hinoki (Kiso cypress) is a high-quality woodworking material sourced from central Japan's Kiso Valley. Its consistent grain makes it perfect for high-end projects.

By understanding the basic concepts of accuracy, strength, and aesthetics, as well as using traditional skills and materials, Japanese artisans can produce joinery that is not only useful and lasting, but also infused with a feeling of beauty and workmanship that lasts generations.

CHAPTER THREE

Types of Japanese Joints

Mortise and Tenon Joints

1. Overview. Mortise and tenon joints are one of the most basic and common forms of joinery in Japanese woodworking. They are made up of two parts: the mortise, a rectangular or square hole cut into one piece of wood, and the tenon, a projecting tongue or tab on the end of another piece of wood that is meant to fit snugly into the mortise.

2. Different types of mortise and tenon joints:

• The through-mortise and tenon connection ensures optimal strength and stability as the tenon travels entirely through the mortise. It is often utilized in heavy-duty applications including wood framing and furniture building.

- The blind or halted mortise and tenon variety allows for a cleaner look on one side of the joint by not extending through the entire thickness of the mortise. This style of connection is often employed in fine furniture and cabinets, where aesthetics are paramount.

- To secure the connection, a wedge is inserted into a slot cut into the end of the tenon after assembly. The wedging movement causes the tenon to expand inside the mortise, resulting in a tight and lasting attachment.

3. Tools and Techniques: • Chisels: Use traditional Japanese chisels, or nomi, for precise mortise and tenon carving.

• Japanese saws, with fine teeth and a pull-stroke cutting motion, are used to cut tenon cheeks and define mortise edges.

• Use marking gauges and layout tools to correctly mark mortise and tenon joints on wood.

Dovetail joints

1. Overview: Dovetail joints have a unique interlocking form that mimics a dove's tail. These joints are highly regarded for their strength, resistance to pulling forces, and esthetic appeal. Dovetail joints are widely employed in Japanese woodworking for furniture, drawer boxes, and ornamental joinery.

2. Types of Dovetail Joints:

• The through dovetail connection creates a symmetrical look with visible tails and pins on both sides of the workpiece. Through dovetails are often utilized in exposed joinery when aesthetics are crucial.

• Half-blind dovetail: This variety hides the tail ends behind a recessed part of the neighboring workpiece, creating a clean and smooth appearance on one side of the connection. Half-blind dovetails are often employed in drawer construction, with the tail ends concealed from view.

• Sliding dovetail joint: One workpiece's tail glides into a groove or dado cut in the matching piece. Sliding dovetails are often used to attach shelves to bookcase sides or tabletops to their bases.

3. Utilize traditional tools and techniques.

• Japanese chisels are used to create dovetail recesses and ensure proper joint fit.

• Japanese pull saws are used to precisely cut dovetail tails and pins, resulting in a tight fit and smooth look.

• Marking tools, like as dovetail markers and gauges, are used to correctly mark the angles and dimensions of dovetail joints on wood.

Japanese artisans may increase the beauty and practicality of their woodworking creations by learning the methods of mortise and tenon joints and dovetail joints.

Half-Lap Joints

1. Overview. Half-lap joints, or halving joints, are a flexible style of joinery employed in Japanese woodworking. They entail eliminating half of the thickness from each of the two pieces of wood to be connected, resulting in a flat surface when the parts are completed. Half-lap joints are popular for their simplicity, robustness, and ease of assembly, making them ideal for a variety of applications such as frame building, box manufacture, and furniture assembly.

2. Use traditional tools and techniques.

- Japanese pull saws are used to cut half-lap joints precisely, resulting in a tight fit and smooth surface.

- Japanese chisels eliminate superfluous material and refine joint edges for a close fit.

- Marking gauges and scribes are used to precisely indicate the size and placement of half-lap joints on wood.

Through-tenon joints

1. Overview: Through-tenon joints are a traditional Japanese joinery style noted for its strength, longevity, and aesthetic appeal. In this style of joint, a tenon extends all the way through a mortise in the next piece of wood, forming a solid and durable connection. Through-tenon joints are often employed in wood framing, furniture

building, and traditional Japanese architecture to give structural support while also enhancing the piece's overall aesthetics.

2. Use traditional tools and techniques.

• Japanese chisels are used to precisely carve out mortises and form tenons, resulting in a tight and smooth connection.

• Japanese saws are used to cut the tenon cheeks and mortise edges, ensuring perfect joint assembly.

• Marking gauges and scribes are used to precisely indicate the size and placement of through-tenon joints on wood.

Other Joints

1. Bridle Joints: • Bridle joints, also known as open mortise and tenon joints, have a notch or groove carved into both pieces of wood to form a stronger and more robust connection. Bridle joints are often used in furniture manufacturing, cabinetry, and wood framing to give structural support and increase the overall strength of the joint.

2. Finger Joints: • Box joints or comb joints are interlocking joinery that connects two pieces of wood at right angles. Finger joints are made up of many interlocking fingers or tabs carved into the ends of two pieces of wood, which provide a strong and sturdy connection. Finger joints are widely used in box building, drawer

manufacture, and furniture assembly because they produce a visually appealing and long-lasting connection that can endure large weights and frequent usage.

Craftsmen who understand the methods of half-lap joints, through-tenon joints, and other forms of Japanese joinery may build strong, durable, and visually appealing connections that improve the aesthetics and functionality of their woodworking creations.

CHAPTER FOUR

Step-by-Step Techniques for Japanese Joinery

Detailed Instructions on Measuring and Cutting Joints Accurately

1. Preliminary planning

• Examine the woodworking project blueprints or specifications to identify the necessary joints and sizes.

• Choose proper tools and materials based on wood species, thickness, and desired finish for cutting joints.

2. Marking: • Use layout tools such marking gauges, combination squares, and knives to correctly mark joint locations and measurements on wood.

- Mark workpieces on the right sides and edges, allowing for wood movement and final assembly.

3. Cutting Tenons: • Use a marking gauge or combination square to measure and mark the length of the tenon at the workpiece's end.

- Create tenon cheeks by cutting along indicated lines with a saw. Cut precisely and properly to provide a snug fit.

- Use a chisel to eliminate superfluous material between the tenon cheeks, ensuring clean and straight edges.

- Ensure the tenon fits snugly in the mortise without gaps. Adjust as needed.

4. Cutting Mortises: • Measure and mark the mortise dimensions on the

mating workpiece to ensure perfect alignment with the tenon.

• Mark the mortise limits using a marking gauge or combination square, ensuring accuracy and consistency.

• Use a drill or chisel to remove waste material from the mortise, staying within the specified borders.

• To guarantee a perfect fit, use a chisel to level off the mortise corners and refine the edges. Test the fit occasionally.

5. Fine-Tuning and Assembly: • After cutting the tenons and mortises to size, use a chisel or hand plane to adjust the fit of the joints and remove any high spots or defects.

- Verify joint alignment by dry-fitting and ensuring no gaps.

- Use the proper adhesive or finish for the joints, following manufacturer recommendations and allowing time for drying or curing.

- Assemble joints with uniform pressure for a tight and solid connection. If required, use clamps or other holding devices to keep the components aligned during assembly.

6. Final Inspection and Adjustment: • After assembly, thoroughly check joints for gaps, misalignments, and other flaws.

- Use hand tools to trim, shave, or sand joints to ensure a flawless fit and finish.

- Finish and assemble the woodworking item as needed after ensuring joint quality.

By following these thorough step-by-step directions for precisely measuring and cutting joints, woodworkers may get exact and dependable results in their Japanese joinery projects, assuring strong, durable, and visually beautiful connections that will last.

Tips for Selecting the Appropriate Joint for Different Woodworking Projects

1. Evaluate functional needs for woodworking projects, including load-bearing capability, durability, and simplicity of assembly.

- Select the appropriate joint for the application, considering load weight, force direction, and expected lifetime.

2. Evaluate aesthetic considerations.

- Consider the final project's visual look, including style, dimensions, and design.

- Choose joints that fit the project's visual aspects, including clean, minimalist lines and detailed detailing.

3. Evaluate Structural Integrity: • Consider the woodworking project's structural needs, such as stability, stiffness, and resistance to stress.

- Select joints with enough strength and stability to sustain the specified load and resist external forces including gravity, movement, and environmental conditions.

4. Consider Wood Movement: • Consider the natural movement and expansion of wood caused by humidity, temperature, and environmental variables.

• Choose joints that allow for wood movement while retaining structural integrity to avoid splitting, warping, or joint failure over time.

5. Balance Complexity and Skill Level:
• Consider your own woodworking abilities and experience level when selecting joints for a project, including precision, accuracy, and complexity.

• Choose joints based on your expertise and comfort level, balancing difficulty and efficiency.

Demonstrations of Assembly Methods and Securing Joints

1. Start by dry-fitting the joint components without adhesives or fasteners to confirm good alignment and fit.

• Conduct test assemblies to ensure proper component fit and allow for any necessary changes before final assembly.

2. Adhesive Application: • Apply woodworking adhesive, such wood glue or epoxy, to the joint components' mating surfaces.

• Use a brush or applicator to uniformly distribute glue and cover joint surfaces.

3. Clamping and Pressure Application: • Apply uniform pressure to the joint

during assembly to ensure a stable connection.

• Position clamps strategically to prevent joint components from slipping during curing.

4. Allow Proper Drying Time: • When using adhesives, follow manufacturer recommendations for drying or curing timeframes. Allow enough time for the junction to set and cure before releasing clamps or applying tension.

• To prevent weakening or compromising the adhesive bond, avoid disrupting the junction during drying.

5. Reinforcement and Finishing: • If needed, add screws, dowels, or mechanical connections to strengthen and stabilize the joint.

- After the joint has completely healed, remove any excess glue and sand or polish the surface for a smooth and seamless look.

By following these assembly method and joint securing demonstrations, woodworkers can ensure that their Japanese joinery projects are assembled with precision, stability, and durability, resulting in high-quality finished pieces that highlight the beauty and craftsmanship of traditional woodworking techniques.

CHAPTER FIVE

Traditional Japanese woodworking projects

Here are some basic traditional Japanese woodworking projects demonstrating different joints:

These projects demonstrate the flexibility and artistry of traditional Japanese carpentry, exhibiting the expert use of numerous joints to build practical and aesthetically pleasing objects that are strongly entrenched in Japanese culture and history.

Tansu Chest

Creating a Tansu Chest, a traditional Japanese storage chest, requires meticulous attention to detail, accuracy, and knowledge of numerous carpentry methods. Here's a step-by-step instructions:

1. Design and Plan:

- Research classic Tansu chest designs, including measurements, proportions, and desirable features like drawers, doors, and compartments.

- Develop a precise design or layout including measurements, joinery methods, and material needs.

2. Material Selection and Preparation: • Use high-quality hardwoods like Japanese cedar (sugi), cypress (hinoki), or keyaki (zelkova) for the chest's construction.

- Mill timber to proper dimensions, assuring straight, square, and consistent parts for assembly.

3. Layout and cut joinery components, such as dovetail joints for corners, mortise and tenon joints for frames, and bridle joints for drawers.

- Use marking gauges and scribes to correctly mark joint locations and measurements on wood.

- Use traditional Japanese hand tools like chisels, saws, and planes to cut joinery components with precision and clean edges.

4. Assemble the Frame and Panels: • Begin by building the chest frame, using dovetail joints to link corners and mortise and tenon joints for rails and stiles.

- Cut and fit panels for sides, back, and top of chest, providing a tight fit inside the frame.

- Use classic joinery methods like tongue and groove or rabbet joints to attach panels to the frame.

5. Drawer and Door Construction: • Build the chest drawers using dovetail joints for corners and bridle joints for the fronts.

• Use mortise and tenon joints for doors to ensure smooth operation and snug fit.

6. Finishing Touches: • Sand all chest surfaces to eliminate rough places and provide a clean finish.

• Use a traditional Japanese finish, such as natural oil or urushi lacquer, to maintain and enhance the wood's inherent beauty.

• Install historic hardware, such iron handles, hinges, and drawer pulls, to enhance the chest's authenticity and practicality.

7. Final Inspection and Adjustments: • Thoroughly check the chest to guarantee tight joints and structural integrity.

• Use hand tools to alter and fine-tune joints for better fit, function, and aesthetics.

8. Celebration and Use: • Celebrate the Tansu chest's completion with friends and family, highlighting its workmanship and utility.

• Use the chest to store and arrange clothes, linens, and other household objects, valuing its beauty and use in daily life.

By following these methods and using traditional Japanese woodworking techniques, you may make a Tansu chest that exudes the timeless beauty and craftsmanship of Japanese woodworking traditions.

Chabudai (Low Dining Table)

Making a Chabudai, a traditional Japanese low dining table, requires precise workmanship and attention to detail. Here's a step-by-step instructions for creating one:

1. Design and Plan:

- Research traditional Chabudai designs to determine dimensions, proportions, and desirable qualities such leg height and tabletop size.

- Develop a precise design or layout including measurements, joinery methods, and material needs.

2. Material selection and preparation.

- Use high-quality hardwoods like Japanese cedar (sugi), cypress (hinoki), or keyaki (zelkova) for the table's construction.

- Mill timber to proper dimensions, assuring straight, square, and consistent parts for assembly.

3. Joinery Layout and Cutting: • Lay out joinery components, such as

mortise and tenon joints for legs and half-lap joints for cross supports.

• Use marking gauges and scribes to correctly mark joint locations and measurements on wood.

• Use traditional Japanese hand tools like chisels, saws, and planes to cut joinery components with precision and clean edges.

4. Assemble Tabletop and Legs: • Begin by connecting the Chabudai's legs to the tabletop using mortise and tenon joints.

• Use half-lap joints to secure cross supports between legs, ensuring stability and strength.

• For a solid structure, use conventional joinery methods like dowels or wooden pegs. • To finish and smooth the Chabudai, sand all surfaces to eliminate rough patches and irregularities.

• Use a traditional Japanese finish, such as natural oil or urushi lacquer, to maintain and enhance the wood's inherent beauty.

• Use a hand plane or scraper to produce clean, chamfered edges on the tabletop and legs, improving its visual appeal.

6. Final Inspection and Adjustment:

• Inspect the Chabudai to verify tight joints and structural integrity.

• Use hand tools to alter and fine-tune joints for better fit, function, and aesthetics.

7. Celebration and Use: • Celebrate the Chabudai's completion with friends and family, highlighting its workmanship and utility.

• Use the Chabudai as a centerpiece for meetings and meals, highlighting its beauty and functionality in daily life.

By following these procedures and using traditional Japanese carpentry methods, you may make a Chabudai that exudes the beauty, simplicity, and usefulness of traditional Japanese design.

Magewappa Bentwood Boxes

Magewappa Bentwood Boxes are made using a unique procedure of bending thin strips of wood to achieve the box's shape. Here's a step-by-step instructions:

1. Material Selection: • Choose a flexible wood species, such Japanese

cedar (sugi) or Japanese cypress (hinoki).

• Choose wood with consistent thickness and straight grain, devoid of knots and other blemishes.

2. Wood Preparation: • Use a bandsaw, table saw, or hand plane to create thin, consistent strips.

• To bend wood strips without cracking or splitting, soak them in water or steam.

• To maintain the appropriate curvature, use weights or clamps to keep the strips in form during drying.

3. Designing the Box Form: • Create a template or mold for the required Magewappa box form and size, taking into account height, width, and depth.

- Bend moistened wood strips around the template or mold, gently overlapping them for a tight seal and snug fit.

- To keep the form and curvature of bentwood strips during drying, use clamps or straps to secure them.

4. Assembly and Joinery: • After drying and retaining form, remove bentwood strips from mold or template.

- Cut bentwood strips at exact angles to make smooth joins during installation.

- Connect the ends of bentwood strips using classic joinery methods like finger joints or mitered joints for a strong fit.

- Apply wood glue to seams and clamp together to make a firm bind.

5. Finishing and reinforcement: • Use tiny wooden dowels or pegs to strengthen and stabilize the Magewappa box joints.

• Sand all box surfaces to achieve a smooth and consistent finish.

• Use a traditional Japanese finish, such as natural oil or urushi lacquer, to maintain and enhance the wood's inherent beauty.

6. Final Inspection and Adjustment:

• Inspect the Magewappa box for tight joints and structural integrity.

• Use hand tools to alter and fine-tune joints for better fit, function, and aesthetics.

7. Celebration and Use: • Celebrate the Magewappa Bentwood Box's completion

with friends and family, highlighting its workmanship and utility.

• Use the box to store and display food, tea leaves, or tiny personal possessions, valuing its beauty and use in daily life.

By following these methods and using traditional Japanese woodworking techniques, you may make a Magewappa Bentwood Box that exudes the beauty, simplicity, and usefulness of traditional Japanese design.

Sawhorses (Kigoroshi)

Creating a traditional Japanese sawhorse, known as a "Kigoroshi," requires basic yet durable construction techniques. Here's a step-by-step instructions:

1. Material Selection: • For the sawhorse, choose robust, straight-

grained hardwoods such Japanese cedar (sugi), cypress (hinoki), or oak.

• Choose wood devoid of knots, flaws, and blemishes for longevity and stability.

2. Design and Plan:

• Determine sawhorse size and height for your woodworking requirements.

• Create a basic sawhorse design that considers leg length, bracing, and stability.

3. Cutting the Components: • Use a saw to cut the sawhorse's major components, which include two pairs of legs and a top rail.

• Ensure legs are similar lengths and top rail fits firmly between them.

4. Layout and Cut Joinery Components:
• Lay out mortise and tenon joints to attach legs to top rail.

• Use marking gauges and scribes to correctly mark joint locations and measurements on wood.

• Use traditional Japanese hand tools like chisels, saws, and planes to cut joinery components with precision and clean edges.

5. Assemble Legs and Top Rail: • Begin by attaching one set of legs to the top rail, placing the tenons into the mortises and ensuring a secure fit.

• Repeat the technique for the second set of legs and the top rail, maintaining tight and secure connections throughout.

- When assembling the sawhorse, use clamps or straps to keep it sturdy and level.

6. Bracing and Reinforcement: • Cut and fit diagonal bracing between sawhorse legs using classic joinery methods like half-lap or mortise and tenon joints.

- Attach the braces securely to the legs and top rail for added stability and support. 7. Final Inspection and Adjustments: • Inspect the sawhorse thoroughly for tight joints and structural integrity.

- Use hand tools to alter and fine-tune joints for better fit, function, and aesthetics.

8. Finish and use:

- Sand the sawhorse to eliminate rough places and achieve a smooth and consistent finish.

- To improve longevity and attractiveness, apply a protective finish like natural oil or wax to the sawhorse.

- Use the sawhorse for woodworking operations like sawing, planing, and assembling, and enjoy its stability and versatility in the workshop.

By following these methods and using traditional Japanese woodworking techniques, you may build a strong and dependable sawhorse suitable for a wide range of woodworking projects.

CHAPTER SIX

Getabako (shoe cabinet)

Creating a Getabako, a traditional Japanese shoe cabinet, requires carpentry expertise and meticulous attention to detail. Here's a step-by-step instructions:

1. Design and Plan:

- Determine shoe cabinet size and design based on shoe storage requirements and available space.

- Create a design with the number of compartments, cabinet size, and other features like doors or drawers.

2. Material Selection: • Use high-quality wood like Japanese cedar (sugi), cypress (hinoki), or keyaki (zelkova) to build the shoe cabinet.

- For sides, shelves, and back panels, use plywood or solid wood planks with sufficient thickness.

3. Cutting and Milling: • Use a table saw or circular saw to cut plywood or solid wood boards to required proportions for cabinet sides, shelves, and back panels.

- Cut top, bottom, and door panel boards to the desired size using a miter saw or hand saw.

4. Joinery: • Lay out joinery components, such as dovetail joints for cabinet corners and mortise and tenon connections for frame and panel doors.

- Use marking gauges and pencils to correctly indicate the position and measurements of joints on wood.

- Use traditional Japanese hand tools like chisels, saws, and planes to cut joinery components with precision and clean edges.

5. Assembly: • Assemble the cabinet's sides, top, bottom, and back panels using dovetail joints for corners and rabbet joints to connect the back panel.

• Build frame and panel doors using mortise and tenon joints for the frame and tongue and groove joints for the panels.

• Use traditional Japanese hinges, such as Soss or knife hinges, to attach the doors to the cabinet for a tight fit and smooth functioning.

6. Install shelves in cabinet using traditional Japanese supports like shelf pins or sliding dovetails.

• Maximize storage space by positioning shelves at suitable heights for various shoe sizes.

7. Finishing: • Sand the shoe cabinet's surfaces to eliminate rough places and provide a clean finish.

- Use a traditional Japanese finish, such as natural oil or urushi lacquer, to maintain and enhance the wood's inherent beauty.

8. Finishing touches: • Use traditional Japanese hardware like drawer pulls or knobs on cabinet doors to enhance the piece's authenticity and utility.

- Inspect the shoe cabinet to verify tight couplings and structural integrity.

9. Use and Enjoy: • Place the shoe cabinet at the entryway to store and arrange your shoes neatly.

- Appreciate the traditional Japanese shoe cabinet for its workmanship and utility in daily life.

By following these methods and using traditional Japanese woodworking techniques, you can make a lovely and useful Getabako shoe cabinet that adds beauty and order to your house.

Irori (Traditional Japanese Hearth)

Creating an Irori, a traditional Japanese fireplace, requires meticulous design and construction to guarantee safety and usefulness. Here's a step-by-step instructions:

1. Design and Plan:

• Select the best placement for the Irori based on ventilation, closeness to flammable items, and ease of access.

• Determine the appropriate size and form for the hearth based on available space and expected usage.

• Create a design that includes the hearth measurements, fire pit height, and any other elements like seats or surrounding stones.

2. Material Selection: • Use fire-resistant materials like firebrick, clay, or stone for the fireplace.

• Use natural stones or bricks for long-lasting and heat-resistant structures.

3. Preparing the Site: • Clear the space for the Irori, eliminating any foliage, waste, or impediments.

• Level the ground and build a strong foundation for the hearth using gravel, sand, or concrete as required.

4. Building the Fire Pit: • Lay firebrick or clay pieces in a circular or square configuration to build the foundation of the fire pit, leaving a central space for ventilation.

• Build the fire pit walls by stacking firebrick or clay blocks and bonding them together with fireproof mortar.

5. Construction of Surrounding Structure:

• Use natural stones or bricks to create a solid and heat-resistant surround for sitting or cooking. • Leave airflow and ventilation apertures in the surrounding structure to avoid smoke or fume collection.

6. Finishing Touches: • Apply a heat-resistant coating or sealer to the hearth surface to prevent damage and improve appearance.

• Use traditional Japanese hardware like hooks or brackets to hang cooking items or pots over the fire.

• Add a roof or canopy over the fireplace for weather protection and a comfortable environment.

7. Final Inspection and Safety Checks: • Thoroughly check the Irori to verify all components are firmly bonded and correctly manufactured.

- Check for damage or wear on the fireplace to ensure safety and operation, and make required repairs or modifications.

8. Use and Enjoyment: • Once completed and inspected, begin utilizing the Irori for traditional Japanese cooking, heating, or socializing.

- Embrace traditional Japanese hospitality by gathering friends and family around the fire for meals, stories, and tea ceremonies.

By following these instructions and using traditional Japanese building methods, you may make a beautiful and useful Irori hearth that will improve the atmosphere and functionality of your house.

Suggestions for incorporating Japanese joinery into woodworks

Incorporating Japanese joinery methods into furniture, cabinets, and other woodworking projects may enhance the elegance, robustness, and traditional workmanship of your works. Here are some specific tips for incorporating Japanese joinery into your woodworking projects.

1. Select appropriate joinery techniques.

• Research Japanese joinery methods, including mortise and tenon, dovetail, and half-lap joints. Each approach has advantages and disadvantages, so choose the ones that best fit your project's design and specifications.

- Evaluate the aesthetic and practical elements of various joinery methods. For example, dovetail joints are recognized for their strength and durability, making them excellent for structural components, while half-lap joints are often employed to create flat surfaces and seamless connections.

2. Design with Joinery in Mind: • Incorporate joinery into your design from the beginning, rather than as an afterthought. Plan the arrangement and placement of joints to improve the overall appearance and structural integrity of the item.

- Try alternative joint configurations and combinations to attain the desired appearance and functionality. Consider employing through-tenon joints for visible connections or hidden dovetail joints to improve strength and stability.

3. Choose High-Quality Materials: • Use hardwoods like Japanese cedar (sugi), cypress (hinoki), or keyaki (zelkova) for woodworking projects. These woods are known for their beauty, durability, and versatility, making them perfect for displaying elaborate joinery.

• When choosing timber for joinery, consider grain orientation and wood properties. Straight, clean grain improves the appearance of joints and provides a firm basis for accurate cutting and fitting.

4. Precision Cutting and Fitting: • Ensure precise measurement, marking, and cutting of joinery components. To obtain clean, precise cuts and tight

joints, use traditional Japanese hand tools such chisels, saws, and planes. Proper technique and sharpening are essential for cutting and shaping joinery. Sharp tools provide cleaner cuts and smoother surfaces, which leads to tighter joints and overall higher workmanship.

5. Learn about traditional Japanese joinery methods, including Kumiko, Tsugite, and Sashimono. These methods may enhance your work with ornamental components and visual intrigue, all while highlighting the elegance of traditional Japanese craftsmanship.

• Incorporate traditional Japanese joinery patterns into furniture and cabinetry designs, whether as freestanding pieces or embellishments to existing methods.

6. Practice and Patience: • Mastering Japanese joinery demands patience and attention to detail. Take the time to practice and experiment with your joinery projects, gradually increasing their complexity and intricacy.

• Embrace errors and seek help from experienced woodworkers, books, films, and workshops. Learning from other people's experiences and criticism can help you improve your joinery abilities and gain more mastery over your woodworking pursuits.

By implementing these recommendations into your woodworking projects, you may improve your skills and produce pieces that demonstrate the timeless beauty and perfection of Japanese joinery methods. Whether you're making furniture, cabinets, or other woodworking projects, Japanese joinery provides limitless opportunities for creativity and expression.